THE
HIDDEN
WORDS

THE
HIDDEN
WORDS

BAHÁ'U'LLÁH

Translated by Shoghi Effendi
with the assistance of some
English friends

BAHÁ'Í
PUBLISHING
WILMETTE, ILLINOIS

Bahá'í Publishing
401 Greenleaf Avenue, Wilmette, Illinois 60091

Printed in China

25 24 23 22   8 7 6 5

Library of Congress Cataloging-in-Publication Data

Bahá'u'lláh, 1817–1892.
 [Kalimat al-maknunah. English]
 The hidden words / Bahá'u'lláh ; translated by Shoghi Effendi, with the assistance of some English friends.
     p. cm.
 Includes index.
 ISBN 978-1-61851-018-1 (alk. paper)
 1. Bahai Faith—Prayers and devotions. I. Shoghi, Effendi. II. Title.
 BP362.K313 2012
 297.9'3822—dc23

                                       2012021249

Cover design by Andrew Johnson
Book design by Patrick Falso

Contents

Introduction

The Word of God in every major religion has been delivered to humankind through His great Prophets. Bahá'u'lláh, Whose name means the "Glory of God," and Whose followers believe Him to be the most recent in the succession of these great Prophets of God, has brought a new revelation for today. His followers, known as Bahá'ís, regard His recorded writings and utterances as holy scripture.

During the forty years of Bahá'u'lláh's ministry (1852–1892)—despite exile from His native land of Iran, bitter religious persecution, and unspeakable physical hardships and suffering—He delivered an immense and glorious revelation that is unique for its breadth as well as its authenticity. For the first time in history, the words of the Prophet have been recorded as He dictated them, sometimes even in His own hand. Many times the circumstances in which they were revealed were also recorded by His amanuensis or by other companions and followers who were in His presence.

Among the vast body of scriptures that Bahá'u'lláh has bequeathed to humanity is The Hidden Words, a collection of 153 gem-like aphorisms He revealed in 1858 while meditating and walking the banks of the Tigris River in Baghdad, Iraq. Composed partly in Arabic and partly in Persian, the book was first translated into English around the beginning of the twentieth century, making it one of the earliest works of Bahá'u'lláh to be made available in the West. It is now one of the best known of Bahá'u'lláh's many works, having been translated into many other languages and distributed virtually all over the world.

The Hidden Words was originally known to Bahá'ís as the "Hidden Book of Fatimah," the daughter of the Prophet Muḥammad and the holiest, most outstanding woman of Islam. According to the traditions of Shiah Islam, Fatimah was deeply stricken with grief after her father's death. The traditions hold that the angel Gabriel visited her and whispered inspiring, consoling words to give her spiritual comfort during a time of extreme anguish.

Bahá'u'lláh Himself has identified The Hidden Words with the words of consolation that were whispered to Fatimah and characterizes it as "that which hath descended from the realm of glory, uttered by the tongue of power and might, and revealed unto the Prophets of old." Bahá'u'lláh states, "We have taken the inner essence thereof and clothed it in the garment of brevity, as a token of grace unto the righteous, that they may stand faithful unto the Covenant of God, may fulfill in their lives His trust, and in the realm of spirit obtain the gem of divine virtue."

This work represents the ethical heart of Bahá'-u'lláh's teachings. In it He has distilled and presented in brief form the spiritual essence of all previous revelations. Addressing myriad spiritual themes including purity, love, kindness, justice, radiance, faithfulness, selflessness, humility, detachment from worldly possessions, wisdom, and nearness to God—to name only a few—The Hidden Words reveals afresh the true foundations of religion. It is, as Bahá'u'lláh says, a "token of grace"—an expression of unmerited divine assistance given to humanity for its spiritual regeneration, a key to understanding the mysteries that surround our spiritual life, and a perfect guide to spiritual growth.

The sincere recitation of these holy verses—priceless gifts of a loving Creator—is a bounty that Bahá'u'lláh promises will have a profound effect on oneself and the world:

Intone, O My servant, the verses of God that have been received by thee, as intoned by them who have drawn nigh unto Him, that the sweetness of thy melody may kindle thine own soul, and attract the hearts of all men. Whoso reciteth, in the privacy of his chamber, the verses revealed by God, the scattering angels of the Almighty shall scatter abroad the fragrance of the words uttered by his mouth, and shall cause the heart of every righteous man to throb. Though he may, at first, remain unaware of its effect, yet the virtue of the grace vouchsafed unto him must needs sooner or later exercise its influence upon his soul. Thus have the mysteries of the Revelation of God been decreed by virtue of the Will of Him Who is the Source of power and wisdom.[1]

---

1. Bahá'u'lláh, *Gleanings from the Writings of Bahá'u'lláh*, trans. Shoghi Effendi (Wilmette, IL: Bahá'í Publishing, 2005), no. 136.2.

THE
HIDDEN
WORDS

He Is the Glory of Glories

*T*his is that which hath descended from the realm of glory, uttered by the tongue of power and might, and revealed unto the Prophets of old. We have taken the inner essence thereof and clothed it in the garment of brevity, as a token of grace unto the righteous, that they may stand faithful unto the Covenant of God, may fulfill in their lives His trust, and in the realm of spirit obtain the gem of divine virtue.

1.

O Son of Spirit!

My first counsel is this: Possess a pure, kindly and radiant heart, that thine may be a sovereignty ancient, imperishable and everlasting.

2.

O Son of Spirit!

The best beloved of all things in My sight is Justice; turn not away therefrom if thou desirest Me, and neglect it not that I may confide in thee. By its aid thou shalt see with thine own eyes and not through the eyes of others, and shalt know of thine own knowledge and not through the knowledge of thy neighbor. Ponder this in thy heart; how it behooveth thee to be. Verily justice is My gift to thee and the sign of My loving-kindness. Set it then before thine eyes.

3.

O Son of Man!
Veiled in My immemorial being and in the ancient eternity of My essence, I knew My love for thee; therefore I created thee, have engraved on thee Mine image and revealed to thee My beauty.

4.

O Son of Man!

I loved thy creation, hence I created thee. Wherefore, do thou love Me, that I may name thy name and fill thy soul with the spirit of life.

5.

O Son of Being!

Love Me, that I may love thee. If thou lovest Me not, My love can in no wise reach thee. Know this, O servant.

6.

O Son of Being!
Thy Paradise is My love; thy heavenly home, reunion with Me. Enter therein and tarry not. This is that which hath been destined for thee in Our kingdom above and Our exalted dominion.

7.

O Son of Man!
If thou lovest Me, turn away from thyself; and if thou seekest My pleasure, regard not thine own; that thou mayest die in Me and I may eternally live in thee.

8.

O Son of Spirit!

There is no peace for thee save by renouncing thyself and turning unto Me; for it behooveth thee to glory in My name, not in thine own; to put thy trust in Me and not in thyself, since I desire to be loved alone and above all that is.

9.

O Son of Being!
My love is My stronghold; he that entereth therein is safe and secure, and he that turneth away shall surely stray and perish.

10.

O Son of Utterance!

Thou art My stronghold; enter therein that thou mayest abide in safety. My love is in thee, know it, that thou mayest find Me near unto thee.

11.

O Son of Being!
Thou art My lamp and My light is in thee. Get thou from it thy radiance and seek none other than Me. For I have created thee rich and have bountifully shed My favor upon thee.

12.

O *Son of Being!*

With the hands of power I made thee and with the fingers of strength I created thee; and within thee have I placed the essence of My light. Be thou content with it and seek naught else, for My work is perfect and My command is binding. Question it not, nor have a doubt thereof.

13.

O Son of Spirit!

I created thee rich, why dost thou bring thyself down to poverty? Noble I made thee, wherewith dost thou abase thyself? Out of the essence of knowledge I gave thee being, why seekest thou enlightenment from anyone beside Me? Out of the clay of love I molded thee, how dost thou busy thyself with another? Turn thy sight unto thyself, that thou mayest find Me standing within thee, mighty, powerful and self-subsisting.

14.

O Son of Man!

Thou art My dominion and My dominion perisheth not; wherefore fearest thou thy perishing? Thou art My light and My light shall never be extinguished; why dost thou dread extinction? Thou art My glory and My glory fadeth not; thou art My robe and My robe shall never be outworn. Abide then in thy love for Me, that thou mayest find Me in the realm of glory.

15.

O *Son of Utterance!*
Turn thy face unto Mine and renounce all save Me; for My sovereignty endureth and My dominion perisheth not. If thou seekest another than Me, yea, if thou searchest the universe forevermore, thy quest will be in vain.

16.

O Son of Light!

Forget all save Me and commune with My spirit. This is of the essence of My command, therefore turn unto it.

17.

O Son of Man! Be thou content with Me and seek no other helper. For none but Me can ever suffice thee.

18.

O Son of Spirit!

Ask not of Me that which We desire not for thee, then be content with what We have ordained for thy sake, for this is that which profiteth thee, if therewith thou dost content thyself.

19.

O *Son of the Wondrous Vision!*
I have breathed within thee a breath of My own Spirit, that thou mayest be My lover. Why hast thou forsaken Me and sought a beloved other than Me?

20.

O Son of Spirit!

My claim on thee is great, it cannot be forgotten. My grace to thee is plenteous, it cannot be veiled. My love has made in thee its home, it cannot be concealed. My light is manifest to thee, it cannot be obscured.

21.

O Son of Man!

Upon the tree of effulgent glory I have hung for thee the choicest fruits, wherefore hast thou turned away and contented thyself with that which is less good? Return then unto that which is better for thee in the realm on high.

22.

O Son of Spirit!

Noble have I created thee, yet thou hast abased thyself. Rise then unto that for which thou wast created.

23.

O Son of the Supreme!
To the eternal I call thee, yet thou dost seek that which perisheth. What hath made thee turn away from Our desire and seek thine own?

24.

O Son of Man!

Transgress not thy limits, nor claim that which beseemeth thee not. Prostrate thyself before the countenance of thy God, the Lord of might and power.

25.

O Son of Spirit!
Vaunt not thyself over the poor, for I lead him on his way and behold thee in thy evil plight and confound thee forevermore.

26.

O Son of Being!

How couldst thou forget thine own faults and busy thyself with the faults of others? Whoso doeth this is accursed of Me.

27.

O Son of Man!
Breathe not the sins of others so long as thou art thyself a sinner. Shouldst thou transgress this command, accursed wouldst thou be, and to this I bear witness.

28.

O Son of Spirit!

Know thou of a truth: He that biddeth men be just and himself committeth iniquity is not of Me, even though he bear My name.

29.

O Son of Being!
Ascribe not to any soul that which thou wouldst not have ascribed to thee, and say not that which thou doest not. This is My command unto thee, do thou observe it.

30.

O Son of Man!

Deny not My servant should he ask anything from thee, for his face is My face; be then abashed before Me.

31.

O Son of Being!
Bring thyself to account each day ere thou art summoned to a reckoning; for death, unheralded, shall come upon thee and thou shalt be called to give account for thy deeds.

32.

O Son of the Supreme!

I have made death a messenger of joy to thee. Wherefore dost thou grieve? I made the light to shed on thee its splendor. Why dost thou veil thyself therefrom?

33.

O Son of Spirit!
With the joyful tidings of light I hail thee: rejoice! To the court of holiness I summon thee; abide therein that thou mayest live in peace forevermore.

34.

O Son of Spirit!

The spirit of holiness beareth unto thee the joyful tidings of reunion; wherefore dost thou grieve? The spirit of power confirmeth thee in His cause; why dost thou veil thyself? The light of His countenance doth lead thee; how canst thou go astray?

35.

O *Son of Man!*
Sorrow not save that thou art far from Us. Rejoice not save that thou art drawing near and returning unto Us.

36.

O Son of Man!

Rejoice in the gladness of thine heart, that thou mayest be worthy to meet Me and to mirror forth My beauty.

37.

O Son of Man!
Divest not thyself of My beauteous robe, and forfeit not thy portion from My wondrous fountain, lest thou shouldst thirst forevermore.

38.

O Son of Being!

Walk in My statutes for love of Me and deny thyself that which thou desirest if thou seekest My pleasure.

39.

O Son of Man!
Neglect not My commandments if thou lovest My beauty, and forget not My counsels if thou wouldst attain My good pleasure.

40.

O Son of Man!

Wert thou to speed through the immensity of space and traverse the expanse of heaven, yet thou wouldst find no rest save in submission to Our command and humbleness before Our Face.

41.

O *Son of Man!*
Magnify My cause that I may reveal unto
thee the mysteries of My greatness and shine upon
thee with the light of eternity.

42.

O Son of Man!
Humble thyself before Me, that I may graciously visit thee. Arise for the triumph of My cause, that while yet on earth thou mayest obtain the victory.

43.

O Son of Being!
Make mention of Me on My earth, that in My heaven I may remember thee, thus shall Mine eyes and thine be solaced.

44.

O Son of the Throne!

Thy hearing is My hearing, hear thou therewith. Thy sight is My sight, do thou see therewith, that in thine inmost soul thou mayest testify unto My exalted sanctity, and I within Myself may bear witness unto an exalted station for thee.

45.

O Son of Being!

Seek a martyr's death in My path, content with My pleasure and thankful for that which I ordain, that thou mayest repose with Me beneath the canopy of majesty behind the tabernacle of glory.

46.

O Son of Man!

Ponder and reflect. Is it thy wish to die upon thy bed, or to shed thy lifeblood on the dust, a martyr in My path, and so become the manifestation of My command and the revealer of My light in the highest paradise? Judge thou aright, O servant!

47.

O Son of Man!

By My beauty! To tinge thy hair with thy blood is greater in My sight than the creation of the universe and the light of both worlds. Strive then to attain this, O servant!

48.

O *Son of Man!*

For everything there is a sign. The sign of love is fortitude under My decree and patience under My trials.

49.

O Son of Man!
The true lover yearneth for tribulation even as doth the rebel for forgiveness and the sinful for mercy.

50.

O Son of Man!

If adversity befall thee not in My path, how canst thou walk in the ways of them that are content with My pleasure? If trials afflict thee not in thy longing to meet Me, how wilt thou attain the light in thy love for My beauty?

51.

O Son of Man!
My calamity is My providence, outwardly it is fire and vengeance, but inwardly it is light and mercy. Hasten thereunto that thou mayest become an eternal light and an immortal spirit. This is My command unto thee, do thou observe it.

52.

O *Son of Man!*

Should prosperity befall thee, rejoice not, and should abasement come upon thee, grieve not, for both shall pass away and be no more.

53.

O Son of Being!

If poverty overtake thee, be not sad; for in time the Lord of wealth shall visit thee. Fear not abasement, for glory shall one day rest on thee.

54.

O Son of Being!
If thine heart be set upon this eternal, imperishable dominion, and this ancient, everlasting life, forsake this mortal and fleeting sovereignty.

55.

O Son of Being!
Busy not thyself with this world, for with fire
We test the gold, and with gold We test Our servants.

56.

O Son of Man!

Thou dost wish for gold and I desire thy freedom from it. Thou thinkest thyself rich in its possession, and I recognize thy wealth in thy sanctity therefrom. By My life! This is My knowledge, and that is thy fancy; how can My way accord with thine?

57.

O Son of Man!
Bestow My wealth upon My poor, that in heaven thou mayest draw from stores of unfading splendor and treasures of imperishable glory. But by My life! To offer up thy soul is a more glorious thing couldst thou but see with Mine eye.

58.

O Son of Man!

The temple of being is My throne; cleanse it of all things, that there I may be established and there I may abide.

59.

O Son of Being!
Thy heart is My home; sanctify it for My descent. Thy spirit is My place of revelation; cleanse it for My manifestation.

60.

O Son of Man!

Put thy hand into My bosom, that I may rise above thee, radiant and resplendent.

61.

O *Son of Man!*

Ascend unto My heaven, that thou mayest obtain the joy of reunion, and from the chalice of imperishable glory quaff the peerless wine.

62.

O Son of Man!

Many a day hath passed over thee whilst thou hast busied thyself with thy fancies and idle imaginings. How long art thou to slumber on thy bed? Lift up thy head from slumber, for the Sun hath risen to the zenith, haply it may shine upon thee with the light of beauty.

63.

O Son of Man!

The light hath shone on thee from the horizon of the sacred Mount and the spirit of enlightenment hath breathed in the Sinai of thy heart. Wherefore, free thyself from the veils of idle fancies and enter into My court, that thou mayest be fit for everlasting life and worthy to meet Me. Thus may death not come upon thee, neither weariness nor trouble.

64.

O Son of Man!

My eternity is My creation, I have created it for thee. Make it the garment of thy temple. My unity is My handiwork; I have wrought it for thee; clothe thyself therewith, that thou mayest be to all eternity the revelation of My everlasting being.

65.

O Son of Man!

My majesty is My gift to thee, and My grandeur the token of My mercy unto thee. That which beseemeth Me none shall understand, nor can anyone recount. Verily, I have preserved it in My hidden storehouses and in the treasuries of My command, as a sign of My loving-kindness unto My servants and My mercy unto My people.

66.

O Children of the Divine and Invisible Essence!

Ye shall be hindered from loving Me and souls shall be perturbed as they make mention of Me. For minds cannot grasp Me nor hearts contain Me.

67.

O Son of Beauty!
By My spirit and by My favor! By My mercy and by My beauty! All that I have revealed unto thee with the tongue of power, and have written for thee with the pen of might, hath been in accordance with thy capacity and understanding, not with My state and the melody of My voice.

68.

O Children of Men!

Know ye not why We created you all from the same dust? That no one should exalt himself over the other. Ponder at all times in your hearts how ye were created. Since We have created you all from one same substance it is incumbent on you to be even as one soul, to walk with the same feet, eat with the same mouth and dwell in the same land, that from your inmost being, by your deeds and actions, the signs of oneness and the essence of detachment may be made manifest. Such is My counsel to you, O concourse of light! Heed ye this counsel that ye may obtain the fruit of holiness from the tree of wondrous glory.

69.

O Ye Sons of Spirit!

Ye are My treasury, for in you I have treasured the pearls of My mysteries and the gems of My knowledge. Guard them from the strangers amidst My servants and from the ungodly amongst My people.

70.

O Son of Him that Stood by His Own Entity in the Kingdom of His Self!

Know thou, that I have wafted unto thee all the fragrances of holiness, have fully revealed to thee My word, have perfected through thee My bounty and have desired for thee that which I have desired for My Self. Be then content with My pleasure and thankful unto Me.

71.

O Son of Man!

Write all that We have revealed unto thee with the ink of light upon the tablet of thy spirit. Should this not be in thy power, then make thine ink of the essence of thy heart. If this thou canst not do, then write with that crimson ink that hath been shed in My path. Sweeter indeed is this to Me than all else, that its light may endure forever.

Part II.—From the Persian

*In the Name of
the Lord of Utterance,
the Mighty.*

1.

O Ye People that Have Minds to Know and Ears to Hear!

The first call of the Beloved is this: O mystic nightingale! Abide not but in the rose garden of the spirit. O messenger of the Solomon of love! Seek thou no shelter except in the Sheba of the well-beloved. O immortal phoenix! dwell not save on the mount of faithfulness. Therein is thy habitation, if on the wings of thy soul thou soarest to the realm of the infinite and seekest to attain thy goal.

2.

O Son of Spirit!

The bird seeketh its nest; the nightingale the charm of the rose; whilst those birds, the hearts of men, content with transient dust, have strayed far from their eternal nest, and with eyes turned towards the slough of heedlessness are bereft of the glory of the divine presence. Alas! How strange and pitiful; for a mere cupful, they have turned away from the billowing seas of the Most High, and remained far from the most effulgent horizon.

3.

O Friend!
In the garden of thy heart plant naught but the rose of love, and from the nightingale of affection and desire loosen not thy hold. Treasure the companionship of the righteous and eschew all fellowship with the ungodly.

4.

O Son of Justice!
Whither can a lover go but to the land of his beloved? and what seeker findeth rest away from his heart's desire? To the true lover reunion is life, and separation is death. His breast is void of patience and his heart hath no peace. A myriad lives he would forsake to hasten to the abode of his beloved.

5.

O Son of Dust!
Verily I say unto thee: Of all men the most negligent is he that disputeth idly and seeketh to advance himself over his brother. Say: O brethren! Let deeds, not words, be your adorning.

6.

O Son of Earth!

Know, verily, the heart wherein the least remnant of envy yet lingers, shall never attain My everlasting dominion, nor inhale the sweet savors of holiness breathing from My kingdom of sanctity.

7.

O Son of Love!

Thou art but one step away from the glorious heights above and from the celestial tree of love. Take thou one pace and with the next advance into the immortal realm and enter the pavilion of eternity. Give ear then to that which hath been revealed by the Pen of Glory.

8.

O Son of Glory!

Be swift in the path of holiness, and enter the heaven of communion with Me. Cleanse thy heart with the burnish of the spirit, and hasten to the court of the Most High.

9.

O Fleeting Shadow! Pass beyond the baser stages of doubt and rise to the exalted heights of certainty. Open the eye of truth, that thou mayest behold the veilless Beauty and exclaim: Hallowed be the Lord, the most excellent of all creators!

10.

O *Son of Desire!*
Give ear unto this: Never shall mortal eye recognize the everlasting Beauty, nor the lifeless heart delight in aught but in the withered bloom. For like seeketh like, and taketh pleasure in the company of its kind.

11.

O Son of Dust!
Blind thine eyes, that thou mayest behold My beauty; stop thine ears, that thou mayest hearken unto the sweet melody of My voice; empty thyself of all learning, that thou mayest partake of My knowledge; and sanctify thyself from riches, that thou mayest obtain a lasting share from the ocean of My eternal wealth. Blind thine eyes, that is, to all save My beauty; stop thine ears to all save My word; empty thyself of all learning save the knowledge of Me; that with a clear vision, a pure heart and an attentive ear thou mayest enter the court of My holiness.

12.

O Man of Two Visions!

Close one eye and open the other. Close one to the world and all that is therein, and open the other to the hallowed beauty of the Beloved.

13.

O My Children!
I fear lest, bereft of the melody of the dove of heaven, ye will sink back to the shades of utter loss, and, never having gazed upon the beauty of the rose, return to water and clay.

14.

O Friends!

Abandon not the everlasting beauty for a beauty that must die, and set not your affections on this mortal world of dust.

15.

O Son of Spirit!
The time cometh, when the nightingale of holiness will no longer unfold the inner mysteries and ye will all be bereft of the celestial melody and of the voice from on high.

16.

O Essence of Negligence! Myriads of mystic tongues find utterance in one speech, and myriads of hidden mysteries are revealed in a single melody; yet, alas, there is no ear to hear, nor heart to understand.

17.

O Comrades!
The gates that open on the Placeless stand wide and the habitation of the loved one is adorned with the lovers' blood, yet all but a few remain bereft of this celestial city, and even of these few, none but the smallest handful hath been found with a pure heart and sanctified spirit.

18.

O Ye Dwellers in the Highest Paradise!

Proclaim unto the children of assurance that within the realms of holiness, nigh unto the celestial paradise, a new garden hath appeared, round which circle the denizens of the realm on high and the immortal dwellers of the exalted paradise. Strive, then, that ye may attain that station, that ye may unravel the mysteries of love from its windflowers and learn the secret of divine and consummate wisdom from its eternal fruits. Solaced are the eyes of them that enter and abide therein!

19.

O My Friends!
Have ye forgotten that true and radiant morn, when in those hallowed and blessed surroundings ye were all gathered in My presence beneath the shade of the tree of life, which is planted in the all-glorious paradise? Awestruck ye listened as I gave utterance to these three most holy words: O friends! Prefer not your will to Mine, never desire that which I have not desired for you, and approach Me not with lifeless hearts, defiled with worldly desires and cravings. Would ye but sanctify your souls, ye would at this present hour recall that place and those surroundings, and the truth of My utterance should be made evident unto all of you.

In the eighth of the most holy lines, in the fifth Tablet of Paradise, He saith:

20.

O Ye That Are Lying as Dead on the Couch of Heedlessness!

Ages have passed and your precious lives are well-nigh ended, yet not a single breath of purity hath reached Our court of holiness from you. Though immersed in the ocean of misbelief, yet with your lips ye profess the one true faith of God. Him whom I abhor ye have loved, and of My foe ye have made a friend. Notwithstanding, ye walk on My earth complacent and self-satisfied, heedless that My earth is weary of you and everything within it shunneth you. Were ye but to open your eyes, ye would, in truth, prefer a myriad griefs unto this joy, and would count death itself better than this life.

21.

O Moving Form of Dust! I desire communion with thee, but thou wouldst put no trust in Me. The sword of thy rebellion hath felled the tree of thy hope. At all times I am near unto thee, but thou art ever far from Me. Imperishable glory I have chosen for thee, yet boundless shame thou hast chosen for thyself. While there is yet time, return, and lose not thy chance.

22.

O Son of Desire!

The learned and the wise have for long years striven and failed to attain the presence of the All-Glorious; they have spent their lives in search of Him, yet did not behold the beauty of His countenance. Thou without the least effort didst attain thy goal, and without search hast obtained the object of thy quest. Yet, notwithstanding, thou didst remain so wrapt in the veil of self, that thine eyes beheld not the beauty of the Beloved, nor did thy hand touch the hem of His robe. Ye that have eyes, behold and wonder.

23.

O Dwellers in the City of Love!
Mortal blasts have beset the everlasting
candle, and the beauty of the celestial Youth is veiled
in the darkness of dust. The chief of the monarchs
of love is wronged by the people of tyranny and the
dove of holiness lies prisoned in the talons of owls.
The dwellers in the pavilion of glory and the celestial
concourse bewail and lament, while ye repose in the
realm of negligence, and esteem yourselves as of the
true friends. How vain are your imaginings!

24.

*O Ye That Are Foolish,
Yet Have a Name to Be Wise!*
Wherefore do ye wear the guise of shepherds, when
inwardly ye have become wolves, intent upon My
flock? Ye are even as the star, which riseth ere the
dawn, and which, though it seem radiant and lumi-
nous, leadeth the wayfarers of My city astray into
the paths of perdition.

25.

O Ye Seeming Fair Yet Inwardly Foul!

Ye are like clear but bitter water, which to outward seeming is crystal pure but of which, when tested by the divine Assayer, not a drop is accepted. Yea, the sunbeam falls alike upon the dust and the mirror, yet differ they in reflection even as doth the star from the earth: nay, immeasurable is the difference!

26.

O My Friend in Word!

Ponder awhile. Hast thou ever heard that friend and foe should abide in one heart? Cast out then the stranger, that the Friend may enter His home.

27.

O *Son of Dust!*
All that is in heaven and earth I have ordained for thee, except the human heart, which I have made the habitation of My beauty and glory; yet thou didst give My home and dwelling to another than Me; and whenever the manifestation of My holiness sought His own abode, a stranger found He there, and, homeless, hastened unto the sanctuary of the Beloved. Notwithstanding I have concealed thy secret and desired not thy shame.

28.

O Essence of Desire!

At many a dawn have I turned from the realms of the Placeless unto thine abode, and found thee on the bed of ease busied with others than Myself. Thereupon, even as the flash of the spirit, I returned to the realms of celestial glory and breathed it not in My retreats above unto the hosts of holiness.

29.

O Son of Bounty!

Out of the wastes of nothingness, with the clay of My command I made thee to appear, and have ordained for thy training every atom in existence and the essence of all created things. Thus, ere thou didst issue from thy mother's womb, I destined for thee two founts of gleaming milk, eyes to watch over thee, and hearts to love thee. Out of My loving-kindness, 'neath the shade of My mercy I nurtured thee, and guarded thee by the essence of My grace and favor. And My purpose in all this was that thou mightest attain My everlasting dominion and become worthy of My invisible bestowals. And yet heedless thou didst remain, and when fully

grown, thou didst neglect all My bounties and oc-
cupied thyself with thine idle imaginings, in such
wise that thou didst become wholly forgetful, and,
turning away from the portals of the Friend didst
abide within the courts of My enemy.

30.

O Bondslave of the World!
Many a dawn hath the breeze of My loving-kindness wafted over thee and found thee upon the bed of heedlessness fast asleep. Bewailing then thy plight it returned whence it came.

31.

O Son of Earth!

Wouldst thou have Me, seek none other than Me; and wouldst thou gaze upon My beauty, close thine eyes to the world and all that is therein; for My will and the will of another than Me, even as fire and water, cannot dwell together in one heart.

32.

O Befriended Stranger!
The candle of thine heart is lighted by the hand of My power, quench it not with the contrary winds of self and passion. The healer of all thine ills is remembrance of Me, forget it not. Make My love thy treasure and cherish it even as thy very sight and life.

33.

O My Brother!

Hearken to the delightsome words of My honeyed tongue, and quaff the stream of mystic holiness from My sugar-shedding lips. Sow the seeds of My divine wisdom in the pure soil of thy heart, and water them with the water of certitude, that the hyacinths of My knowledge and wisdom may spring up fresh and green in the sacred city of thy heart.

34.

O Dwellers of My Paradise!
With the hands of loving-kindness I have planted in the holy garden of paradise the young tree of your love and friendship, and have watered it with the goodly showers of My tender grace; now that the hour of its fruiting is come, strive that it may be protected, and be not consumed with the flame of desire and passion.

35.

O My Friends!

Quench ye the lamp of error, and kindle within your hearts the everlasting torch of divine guidance. For ere long the assayers of mankind shall, in the holy presence of the Adored, accept naught but purest virtue and deeds of stainless holiness.

36.

O Son of Dust!
The wise are they that speak not unless they obtain a hearing, even as the cup-bearer, who proffereth not his cup till he findeth a seeker, and the lover who crieth not out from the depths of his heart until he gazeth upon the beauty of his beloved. Wherefore sow the seeds of wisdom and knowledge in the pure soil of the heart, and keep them hidden, till the hyacinths of divine wisdom spring from the heart and not from mire and clay.

In the first line of the Tablet it is recorded and written, and within the sanctuary of the tabernacle of God is hidden:

37.

O My Servant!
Abandon not for that which perisheth an everlasting dominion, and cast not away celestial sovereignty for a worldly desire. This is the river of everlasting life that hath flowed from the wellspring of the pen of the merciful; well is it with them that drink!

38.

O Son of Spirit!
Burst thy cage asunder, and even as the phoenix of love soar into the firmament of holiness. Renounce thyself and, filled with the spirit of mercy, abide in the realm of celestial sanctity.

39.

O Offspring of Dust!

Be not content with the ease of a passing day, and deprive not thyself of everlasting rest. Barter not the garden of eternal delight for the dust-heap of a mortal world. Up from thy prison ascend unto the glorious meads above, and from thy mortal cage wing thy flight unto the paradise of the Placeless.

40.

O My Servant!
Free thyself from the fetters of this world, and loose thy soul from the prison of self. Seize thy chance, for it will come to thee no more.

41.

O Son of My Handmaid!

Didst thou behold immortal sovereignty, thou wouldst strive to pass from this fleeting world. But to conceal the one from thee and to reveal the other is a mystery which none but the pure in heart can comprehend.

42.

O My Servant!
Purge thy heart from malice and, innocent of envy, enter the divine court of holiness.

43.

O My Friends!
Walk ye in the ways of the good pleasure of the Friend, and know that His pleasure is in the pleasure of His creatures. That is: no man should enter the house of his friend save at his friend's pleasure, nor lay hands upon his treasures nor prefer his own will to his friend's, and in no wise seek an advantage over him. Ponder this, ye that have insight!

44.

O Companion of My Throne!
Hear no evil, and see no evil, abase not thyself, neither sigh and weep. Speak no evil, that thou mayest not hear it spoken unto thee, and magnify not the faults of others that thine own faults may not appear great; and wish not the abasement of anyone, that thine own abasement be not exposed. Live then the days of thy life, that are less than a fleeting moment, with thy mind stainless, thy heart unsullied, thy thoughts pure, and thy nature sanctified, so that, free and content, thou mayest put away this mortal frame, and repair unto the mystic paradise and abide in the eternal kingdom forevermore.

45.

*A*las! Alas!
O Lovers of Worldly Desire!

Even as the swiftness of lightning ye have passed by the Beloved One, and have set your hearts on satanic fancies. Ye bow the knee before your vain imagining, and call it truth. Ye turn your eyes towards the thorn, and name it a flower. Not a pure breath have ye breathed, nor hath the breeze of detachment been wafted from the meadows of your hearts. Ye have cast to the winds the loving counsels of the Beloved and have effaced them utterly from the tablet of your hearts, and even as the beasts of the field, ye move and have your being within the pastures of desire and passion.

46.

O Brethren in the Path!
Wherefore have ye neglected the mention of the Loved One, and kept remote from His holy presence? The essence of beauty is within the peerless pavilion, set upon the throne of glory, whilst ye busy yourselves with idle contentions. The sweet savors of holiness are breathing and the breath of bounty is wafted, yet ye are all sorely afflicted and deprived thereof. Alas for you and for them that walk in your ways and follow in your footsteps!

47.

O Children of Desire!
Put away the garment of vainglory, and divest yourselves of the attire of haughtiness.

In the third of the most holy lines writ and recorded in the Ruby Tablet by the pen of the unseen this is revealed:

48.

O Brethren!
Be forbearing one with another and set not your affections on things below. Pride not yourselves in your glory, and be not ashamed of abasement. By My beauty! I have created all things from dust, and to dust will I return them again.

49.

O Children of Dust!

Tell the rich of the midnight sighing of the poor, lest heedlessness lead them into the path of destruction, and deprive them of the Tree of Wealth. To give and to be generous are attributes of Mine; well is it with him that adorneth himself with My virtues.

50.

O Quintessence of Passion!
Put away all covetousness and seek contentment; for the covetous hath ever been deprived, and the contented hath ever been loved and praised.

51.

O Son of My Handmaid!

Be not troubled in poverty nor confident in riches, for poverty is followed by riches, and riches are followed by poverty. Yet to be poor in all save God is a wondrous gift, belittle not the value thereof, for in the end it will make thee rich in God, and thus thou shalt know the meaning of the utterance, "In truth ye are the poor," and the holy words, "God is the all-possessing," shall even as the true morn break forth gloriously resplendent upon the horizon of the lover's heart, and abide secure on the throne of wealth.

52.

O *Children of Negligence and Passion!*

Ye have suffered My enemy to enter My house and have cast out My friend, for ye have enshrined the love of another than Me in your hearts. Give ear to the sayings of the Friend and turn towards His paradise. Worldly friends, seeking their own good, appear to love one the other, whereas the true Friend hath loved and doth love you for your own sakes; indeed He hath suffered for your guidance countless afflictions. Be not disloyal to such a Friend, nay rather hasten unto Him. Such is the daystar of the word of truth and faithfulness, that hath dawned above the horizon of the pen of the Lord of all names. Open your ears that ye may hearken unto the word of God, the Help in peril, the Self-Existent.

53.

O Ye that Pride Yourselves on Mortal Riches!

Know ye in truth that wealth is a mighty barrier between the seeker and his desire, the lover and his beloved. The rich, but for a few, shall in no wise attain the court of His presence nor enter the city of content and resignation. Well is it then with him, who, being rich, is not hindered by his riches from the eternal kingdom, nor deprived by them of imperishable dominion. By the Most Great Name! The splendor of such a wealthy man shall illuminate the dwellers of heaven even as the sun enlightens the people of the earth!

54.

O Ye Rich Ones on Earth! The poor in your midst are My trust; guard ye My trust, and be not intent only on your own ease.

55.

O Son of Passion!
Cleanse thyself from the defilement of riches
and in perfect peace advance into the realm of poverty; that from the wellspring of detachment thou
mayest quaff the wine of immortal life.

56.

O My Son!

The company of the ungodly increaseth sorrow, whilst fellowship with the righteous cleanseth the rust from off the heart. He that seeketh to commune with God, let him betake himself to the companionship of His loved ones; and he that desireth to hearken unto the word of God, let him give ear to the words of His chosen ones.

57.

O Son of Dust!

Beware! Walk not with the ungodly and seek not fellowship with him, for such companionship turneth the radiance of the heart into infernal fire.

58.

O Son of My Handmaid!

Wouldst thou seek the grace of the Holy Spirit, enter into fellowship with the righteous, for he hath drunk the cup of eternal life at the hands of the immortal Cupbearer and even as the true morn doth quicken and illumine the hearts of the dead.

59.

O Heedless Ones!
Think not the secrets of hearts are hidden, nay, know ye of a certainty that in clear characters they are engraved and are openly manifest in the holy Presence.

60.

O Friends!
Verily I say, whatsoever ye have concealed within your hearts is to Us open and manifest as the day; but that it is hidden is of Our grace and favor, and not of your deserving.

61.

O Son of Man!
A dewdrop out of the fathomless ocean of My mercy I have shed upon the peoples of the world, yet found none turn thereunto, inasmuch as everyone hath turned away from the celestial wine of unity unto the foul dregs of impurity, and, content with mortal cup, hath put away the chalice of immortal beauty. Vile is that wherewith he is contented.

62.

O *Son of Dust!*
Turn not away thine eyes from the matchless wine of the immortal Beloved, and open them not to foul and mortal dregs. Take from the hands of the divine Cupbearer the chalice of immortal life, that all wisdom may be thine, and that thou mayest hearken unto the mystic voice calling from the realm of the invisible. Cry aloud, ye that are of low aim! Wherefore have ye turned away from My holy and immortal wine unto evanescent water?

From the Persian

63.

O Ye Peoples of the World!
Know, verily, that an unforeseen calamity followeth you, and grievous retribution awaiteth you. Think not that which ye have committed hath been effaced in My sight. By My beauty! All your doings hath My pen graven with open characters upon tablets of chrysolite.

64.

O Oppressors on Earth!

Withdraw your hands from tyranny, for I have pledged Myself not to forgive any man's injustice. This is My covenant which I have irrevocably decreed in the preserved tablet and sealed with My seal of glory.

65.

O Rebellious Ones! My forbearance hath emboldened you and My long-suffering hath made you negligent, in such wise that ye have spurred on the fiery charger of passion into perilous ways that lead unto destruction. Have ye thought Me heedless or that I was unaware?

66.

O Emigrants!

The tongue I have designed for the mention of Me, defile it not with detraction. If the fire of self overcome you, remember your own faults and not the faults of My creatures, inasmuch as every one of you knoweth his own self better than he knoweth others.

67.

O Children of Fancy! Know, verily, that while the radiant dawn breaketh above the horizon of eternal holiness, the satanic secrets and deeds done in the gloom of night shall be laid bare and manifest before the peoples of the world.

68.

O *Weed that Springeth Out of Dust!*

Wherefore have not these soiled hands of thine touched first thine own garment, and why with thine heart defiled with desire and passion dost thou seek to commune with Me and to enter My sacred realm? Far, far are ye from that which ye desire.

69.

O Children of Adam!
Holy words and pure and goodly deeds ascend unto the heaven of celestial glory. Strive that your deeds may be cleansed from the dust of self and hypocrisy and find favor at the court of glory; for ere long the assayers of mankind shall, in the holy presence of the Adored One, accept naught but absolute virtue and deeds of stainless purity. This is the daystar of wisdom and of divine mystery that hath shone above the horizon of the divine will. Blessed are they that turn thereunto.

70.

O Son of Worldliness!

Pleasant is the realm of being, wert thou to attain thereto; glorious is the domain of eternity, shouldst thou pass beyond the world of mortality; sweet is the holy ecstasy if thou drinkest of the mystic chalice from the hands of the celestial Youth. Shouldst thou attain this station, thou wouldst be freed from destruction and death, from toil and sin.

71.

O My Friends!
Call ye to mind that covenant ye have entered into with Me upon Mount Párán, situate within the hallowed precincts of Zamán. I have taken to witness the concourse on high and the dwellers in the city of eternity, yet now none do I find faithful unto the covenant. Of a certainty pride and rebellion have effaced it from the hearts, in such wise that no trace thereof remaineth. Yet knowing this, I waited and disclosed it not.

72.

O My Servant!

Thou art even as a finely tempered sword concealed in the darkness of its sheath and its value hidden from the artificer's knowledge. Wherefore come forth from the sheath of self and desire that thy worth may be made resplendent and manifest unto all the world.

73.

O *My Friend!*
Thou art the daystar of the heavens of My holiness, let not the defilement of the world eclipse thy splendor. Rend asunder the veil of heedlessness, that from behind the clouds thou mayest emerge resplendent and array all things with the apparel of life.

74.

O Children of Vainglory!

For a fleeting sovereignty ye have abandoned My imperishable dominion, and have adorned yourselves with the gay livery of the world and made of it your boast. By My beauty! All will I gather beneath the one-colored covering of the dust and efface all these diverse colors save them that choose My own, and that is purging from every color.

75.

O Children of Negligence!
Set not your affections on mortal sovereignty and rejoice not therein. Ye are even as the unwary bird that with full confidence warbleth upon the bough; till of a sudden the fowler Death throws it upon the dust, and the melody, the form and the color are gone, leaving not a trace. Wherefore take heed, O bondslaves of desire!

76.

O Son of My Handmaid!

Guidance hath ever been given by words, and now it is given by deeds. Everyone must show forth deeds that are pure and holy, for words are the property of all alike, whereas such deeds as these belong only to Our loved ones. Strive then with heart and soul to distinguish yourselves by your deeds. In this wise We counsel you in this holy and resplendent tablet.

From the Persian

77.

O Son of Justice!
In the night-season the beauty of the immortal Being hath repaired from the emerald height of fidelity unto the Sadratu'l-Muntahá, and wept with such a weeping that the concourse on high and the dwellers of the realms above wailed at His lamenting. Whereupon there was asked, Why the wailing and weeping? He made reply: As bidden I waited expectant upon the hill of faithfulness, yet inhaled not from them that dwell on earth the fragrance of fidelity. Then summoned to return I beheld, and lo! certain doves of holiness were sore tried within the claws of the dogs of earth. Thereupon the Maid of heaven hastened forth unveiled and resplendent

from Her mystic mansion, and asked of their names, and all were told but one. And when urged, the first letter thereof was uttered, whereupon the dwellers of the celestial chambers rushed forth out of their habitation of glory. And whilst the second letter was pronounced they fell down, one and all, upon the dust. At that moment a voice was heard from the inmost shrine: "Thus far and no farther." Verily We bear witness to that which they have done and now are doing.

78.

O Son of My Handmaid!

Quaff from the tongue of the merciful the stream of divine mystery, and behold from the dayspring of divine utterance the unveiled splendor of the daystar of wisdom. Sow the seeds of My divine wisdom in the pure soil of the heart, and water them with the waters of certitude, that the hyacinths of knowledge and wisdom may spring up fresh and green from the holy city of the heart.

79.

O Son of Desire!

How long wilt thou soar in the realms of desire? Wings have I bestowed upon thee, that thou mayest fly to the realms of mystic holiness and not the regions of satanic fancy. The comb, too, have I given thee that thou mayest dress My raven locks, and not lacerate My throat.

80.

O My Servants!
Ye are the trees of My garden; ye must give forth goodly and wondrous fruits, that ye yourselves and others may profit therefrom. Thus it is incumbent on every one to engage in crafts and professions, for therein lies the secret of wealth, O men of understanding! For results depend upon means, and the grace of God shall be all-sufficient unto you. Trees that yield no fruit have been and will ever be for the fire.

81.

O My Servant!

The basest of men are they that yield no fruit on earth. Such men are verily counted as among the dead, nay better are the dead in the sight of God than those idle and worthless souls.

82.

O My Servant!
The best of men are they that earn a livelihood by their calling and spend upon themselves and upon their kindred for the love of God, the Lord of all worlds.

The mystic and wondrous Bride, hidden ere this beneath the veiling of utterance, hath now, by the grace of God and His divine favor, been made manifest even as the resplendent light shed by the beauty of the Beloved. I bear witness, O friends! that the favor is complete, the argument fulfilled, the proof manifest and the evidence established. Let it now be seen what your endeavors in the path of detachment will reveal. In this wise hath the divine favor been fully vouchsafed unto you and unto them that are in heaven and on earth. All praise to God, the Lord of all Worlds.

Appendix

ABOUT BAHÁ'U'LLÁH

Bahá'u'lláh, whose name means in Arabic "the Glory of God," is the founder of the Bahá'í Faith. His followers, known as Bahá'ís, believe Him to be the latest in a line of great Prophets, or Manifestations of God, that includes Abraham, Moses, Zoroaster, Jesus, and Muḥammad.

Born Mírzá Ḥusayn-'Alí on 12 November 1817 in Tehran, the capital of Persia (now Iran), Bahá'u'lláh was a member of a wealthy noble family that could trace its ancestry to the ruling dynasties of Persia's imperial past. Though He was invited to follow His father in government service in a ministerial position that would have ensured a life of wealth and luxury, He had no interest in politics. He chose instead to devote Himself to philanthropic endeavors and to an undertaking that has gradually captured the imagination and loyalty of some five million people from virtually every race, culture, class, and nation on earth. The undertaking is today embodied in the Bahá'í Faith, the youngest of the independent world religions.

In 1844 Bahá'u'lláh embraced the cause of a young merchant from Shiraz known as the Báb (Gate), Who was advancing a claim that the advent of a universal Prophet, the Promised One of all religions—"Him Whom God shall make manifest"—was imminent and that His advent would usher in an era of universal peace and initiate a new cycle in the religious history of humankind. This occurred during a period marked by social upheaval and messianic expectation around the globe. Believers from many faith traditions were seeking guidance from their scriptures about the fulfillment of prophecies signaling the end of human history. Many Christians felt the return of Christ was near at hand. Shiah Muslims speculated about the return of the Twelfth Imam (also known as the Qá'im, or "the one who shall arise from the family of Muḥammad").

The Báb's announcement provoked swift and severe responses from both church and state in His native land. They believed that Muḥammad was the last and final Prophet of God; thus the Báb and His followers, known as Bábís, were seen as a dangerous heretical movement that must be stopped. The Báb was arrested, beaten, and imprisoned, and eventually He was publicly executed in 1850. Some twenty thousand of His followers were killed, many after enduring heinous torture.

Bahá'u'lláh quickly became a leading supporter and defender of the Báb's cause. As a result, He, too, was assailed by the same forces of ignorance and fanaticism that had imprisoned and executed the Báb. He was cast into the infamous Black Pit of Tehran, an underground dungeon from which few escaped with their lives. There, surrounded by thieves and murderers, He was fettered with heavy shackles and chains that cut into His flesh. He and the cause He so vigorously espoused were expected to perish. Yet it was there in the Black Pit that Bahá'u'lláh received the first intimations of His own mission. Many years later, near the end of His life, Bahá'u'lláh described the experience as follows:

> One night, in a dream, these exalted words were heard on every side: "Verily, We shall render Thee victorious by Thyself and by Thy Pen.

Grieve Thou not for that which hath befallen Thee, neither be Thou afraid, for Thou art in safety. Erelong will God raise up the treasures of the earth—men who will aid Thee through Thyself and through Thy Name, wherewith God hath revived the hearts of such as have recognized Him."

Bahá'u'lláh further described the experience, saying,

During the days I lay in the prison of Ṭihrán, though the galling weight of the chains and the stench-filled air allowed Me but little sleep, still in those infrequent moments of slumber I felt as if something flowed from the crown of My head over My breast, even as a mighty torrent that precipitateth itself upon the earth from the summit of a lofty mountain. Every limb of My body would, as a result, be set afire. At such moments My tongue recited what no man could bear to hear.

Through the experience of divine revelation amidst the horror, agony, and gloom of the Black Pit, Bahá'u'lláh began to understand His mission and its relationship to the Báb's prophetic words regarding "Him Whom God shall make manifest."

Bahá'u'lláh survived His imprisonment and was released after four months; however, the remaining forty years of His life were marked by severe hardships in the form of exile, further imprisonment, and unrelenting persecution.

Upon His release from prison, Bahá'u'lláh and His family were banished from Persia. He was first exiled to Baghdad, Iraq, and from there He was later banished to Constantinople (Istanbul), then Adrianople (Edirne, Turkey), and finally to the prison-city of Acre, Israel, where He remained for over twenty-four years until His passing on 29 May 1892.

During the course of His exiles, Bahá'u'lláh wrote voluminously, expounding the principles of His faith, formulating its laws and ordinances, proclaiming His message to the kings and rulers of the world, and calling upon them to turn to God and reign with justice.

The aim of Bahá'u'lláh is not to abolish but to fulfill the revelations of the past; to reconcile, rather than accentuate, the divergencies of conflicting creeds; to restate the basic truths of the world's major religions in a manner that conforms to the needs and maturity of the age in which we live; and to herald the approach of an age in which the peace of the planet will be permanently ensured.

The main thrust of His message is unity. He taught that there is only one God, that all of the world's religions represent one changeless and eternal Faith of God, and that all humanity is one race, destined in the fullness of time to live in peace and harmony. He proclaims that the ages of the infancy and childhood of the human race are past, that the convulsions associated with its present stage of adolescence are gradually and painfully preparing it to reach the stage of adulthood, and are heralding the approach of that Age of Ages when swords will be beaten into plowshares, when the Kingdom of God promised by Jesus will have been established, and the peace and prosperity of the entire planet will be definitely and permanently ensured. He proclaims the necessity and inevitability of the unification of humankind, asserting that it is gradually approaching and that nothing short of the spirit of God, working through His chosen Mouthpiece in this day, can ultimately succeed in bringing it about.

Bahá'u'lláh enjoins on His followers the primary duty of an unfettered search for truth, condemns all forms of prejudice and superstition, declares the purpose of religion to be the promotion of friendship and harmony, proclaims the essential harmony of science and religion, and recognizes religion as the foremost agency for the orderly progress of society. He asserts the principle of equal rights, opportunities, and privileges for women and men; insists on compulsory education; declares the necessity of eliminating extremes of poverty and wealth; abolishes the institution of priesthood; prohibits slavery, asceticism, begging, and monasticism; prescribes monogamy; discourages divorce; emphasizes the necessity of strict obedience to one's government; exalts any work performed in the spirit of service to the level of worship; urges the creation or selection of an auxiliary international language; and delineates the outlines of those institutions that must establish and perpetuate the general peace of mankind.

Bahá'u'lláh does not claim that His own revelation is to be the last revelation from God. He promises that a larger measure of the truth that He has been commissioned by God to bestow on humanity will be disclosed at future stages of its constant and ever-advancing evolution.

Index

Note: Locators preceded by "A" refer to Arabic Hidden Words numbers. Those preceded by "P" refer to Persian Hidden Words numbers. Locators not preceded by a letter refer to page numbers.

C

D

I

J

K

L

U

ungodly
    fellowship with, P3, P56, P57
    guarding God's mysteries from, A69
unity of God, A64

V

vain imaginings. *See* idle imaginings
vainglory, P47
victory, A42
virtue, P35, P49

W

wealth
    as barrier, P53
    cleansing self from, P55
    followed by poverty, P51
    as freedom from material world, A56
    and giving to poor, A57
    secrets of, P80
    Tree of, P49
wealthy people, in kingdom of God, P53
wickedness, A28, P24, P25
will of God
    contentment with, A45, A50, A70
    giving preference to, P19, P31

Bahá'í Publishing
and the Bahá'í Faith

Bahá'í Publishing produces books based on the teachings of the Bahá'í Faith. Founded nearly 160 years ago, the Bahá'í Faith has spread to some 235 nations and territories and is now accepted by more than five million people. The word "Bahá'í" means "follower of Bahá'u'lláh." Bahá'u'lláh, the Founder of the Bahá'í Faith, asserted that He is the Messenger of God for all of humanity in this day. The cornerstone of His teachings is the establishment of the spiritual unity of humankind, which will be achieved by personal transformation and the application of clearly identified spiritual principles. Bahá'ís also believe that there is but one religion and that all the Messengers of God—among them Abraham, Zoroaster, Moses, Krishna, Buddha, Jesus, and Muḥammad—have progressively revealed its nature. Together, the world's great religions are expressions of a single, unfolding divine plan. Human beings, not God's Messengers, are the source of religious divisions, prejudices, and hatreds.

The Bahá'í Faith is not a sect or denomination of another religion, nor is it a cult or a social movement. Rather, it is a globally recognized independent world religion founded on new books of scripture revealed by Bahá'u'lláh.

Bahá'í Publishing is an imprint of the National Spiritual Assembly of the Bahá'ís of the United States.

For more information about the Bahá'í Faith,
or to contact the Bahá'ís near you, visit
www.us.bahai.org
or call
1-800-22-UNITE

Other Books
Available from
Bahá'í Publishing

RETRIEVING OUR SPIRITUAL HERITAGE
Bahá'í Chair for World Peace:
Lectures and Essays, 1994–2005
Suheil Bushrui
$20.00 US / $22.00 CAN
Hardcover
ISBN 978-1-61851-016-7

A collection of lectures and essays that place interfaith dialogue, the oneness of humanity, and the human spirit at the heart of public discourse.

In *Retrieving Our Spiritual Heritage,* Professor Bushrui calls for interfaith dialog and focuses on some of the timeless shared values of many of the world's religions—such as love, selflessness, and generosity—but also delves into how these values can be applied to the many conflicts and crises facing the world today. Covering such topics as education, globalization, peace, and the environment, Professor Bushrui evokes the timeless wisdom of the world's religions as well as the voices of the poets and scholars of the past, addressing his subject matter at the level of high principle and universal values. The result is a deeply moving and thought-provoking call to humanity to place the human spirit at the heart of discourse concerning the vital issues of our time.

TALKS BY 'ABDU'L-BAHÁ
THE SPIRIT OF CHRIST
'Abdu'l-Bahá
$14.00 US / $16.00 CAN
Hardcover
ISBN 978-1-61851-020-4

A spiritually uplifting and thought-provoking collection of talks that pay tribute to the spirit of Jesus Christ and the significance of His teachings and station.

Talks by 'Abdu'l-Bahá: The Spirit of Christ is a collection of talks given by 'Abdu'l-Bahá during his historic journey through Europe and North America in 1911 and 1912. As the son and appointed successor of Bahá'u'lláh, the Prophet and Founder of the Bahá'í Faith, 'Abdu'l-Bahá spoke extensively to a wide range of audiences and offered profound insights on a diversity of subjects. This volume specifically highlights talks that deal with the spirit of Christ, and the impact that His life and teachings had on the world. In these talks, readers will find glowing tributes to the station of Christ, Whom Bahá'ís revere as a divinely inspired Messenger of God.

BAHÁ'Í BASICS
A Guide to the Beliefs, Practices, and History
of the Bahá'í Faith
Frances Worthington
$14.00 US / $16.00 CAN
Trade Paper
ISBN 978-1-61851-017-4

An introduction to the Bahá'í Faith that covers the basic teach-
ings, principles, and history of the Faith in an easy-to-use Q&A
format.

In *Bahá'í Basics,* author Frances Worthington uses a simple
and accessible format that highlights the clarity with which
many of the topics associated with the Bahá'í Faith are dis-
cussed. The result is a basic and informational introduction
to what is one of the fastest growing religions in the world. In
most cases the answers are presented using direct quotations
from the central figures of the Faith, including Bahá'u'lláh,
the Báb, 'Abdu'l-Bahá, and Shoghi Effendi. Readers will find
themselves well-informed after reading this concise, well-
organized introduction, which provides clear, straightforward
answers to the basic questions that arise when investigating a
new religion.

SPIRIT OF FAITH
OBEDIENCE TO GOD
Bahá'í Publishing
$12.00 US / $14.00 CAN
Hardcover
ISBN 978-1-61851-019-8

A selection of uplifting prayers and writings that explores the concept of obedience to God and how it relates to our spiritual development and well-being.

Spirit of Faith: Obedience to God is a compilation of Bahá'í writings that deal with the subject of obedience to God. From a Bahá'í perspective, the Prophets or Manifestations of God, the Founders of the world's great religions, are as divine Physicians Whose laws, teachings, and admonitions contain the remedy for the ailments of mankind. To follow the teachings and observe the laws prescribed by the Manifestation of God for the day in which we live is, from a Bahá'í perspective, to fulfill a major part of our duty as human beings and to align ourselves with the divine guidance available to us. From this perspective, obedience can be seen as a source of empowerment and as the core of personal spiritual development.